T0028442

ANTHEM SPEED

Kuhl House Poets
Mark Levine and Emily Wilson, series editors

ANTHEM SPEED

Christopher Bolin

University of Iowa Press · *Iowa City*

University of Iowa Press, Iowa City 52242
Copyright © 2023 by Christopher Bolin
uipress.uiowa.edu
Printed in the United States of America
Design by Sara T. Sauers
Printed on acid-free paper

No part of this book may be reproduced or used in any form or
by any means without permission in writing from the publisher.
All reasonable steps have been taken to contact copyright
holders of material used in this book. The publisher would be
pleased to make suitable arrangements with any whom it has
not been possible to reach.

Library of Congress Cataloging-in-Publication Data
Names: Bolin, Christopher, author.
Title: Anthem Speed / Christopher Bolin.
Description: Iowa City: University of Iowa Press, [2023] |
    Series: Kuhl House Poets
Identifiers: LCCN 2023009362 (print) |
    LCCN 2023009363 (ebook) |
    ISBN 9781609389215 (paperback) |
    ISBN 9781609389222 (ebook)
Subjects: LCGFT: Poetry.
Classification: LCC PS3602.O6533 A84 2023 (print) |
    LCC PS3602.O6533 (ebook) |
    DDC 811/.6—dc23/eng/20230228
LC record available at https://lccn.loc.gov/2023009362
LC ebook record available at https://lccn.loc.gov/2023009363

for Kristin, for Finn

CONTENTS

ANTHEM SPEED

Mendicant's Song

he told us to close our eyes and press their lids and
Hubble images

                       appeared: and our breathlessness arose in our proximity
              to them; and the mind was the seventh summer

of an unfound planet;
            until the mind was the fruit   dusted

by antlered collisions, below,
            and the grafted branch—(over which they fought) could not

support the dust   or a tongue's tip of buck's spittle—

and its cracking turned the injured buck
from its retreat

            as the branch felled
            the other buck and both remained un-scavenged

by the selves conjured to carry the injured
toward the eighth-
summer's

light;

The Absence Activities

checking core-samples   for snow compressed by explorers
       and shifting the drilling

northward
to measure the weight they lost;

air-traffic over the arctic
      leaving contrails as the core-
       samples   of Russian metals

that never arrive;
among

the disinformation of the distress feeds

a pilot hears his coordinates
being called by other planes;

       and with animal collars transmitting
       on these frequencies

       we run ice-depth

tests
by

feeding wolves;

Borderlands

reliquary glass distorting its saint's reach;
and the heights of animals healed; and the chance
they grazed the high rocks   of the hermitage
bare; or searched repairs
for salt from the stonemason's hands
who stacked the stones in cloth
to sift the talc   across the pilgrims' trails

and his calves: still white with talc
or bleeding and clotting in talc
where the fabric tore;

and the sun-motes—above medics' kits
of sterile fibers made—

frenzied by the medics' words
into fusion

simulations
smuggled back and forth

above the wounded;

Encounters in Digital Light

first frost
in the container-

ship

stacks
and the plum-

bruised

mouths
of the deer and

first frost

whitening
the wire

to or from

the tree-
stakes

tensioning
belief; first frost

or wind
tightening

fishing-line
nests

and rattling
the lures

in the cliffs
casting

eyelet-
circled

light; first
frost in the

shadows

propelling the
sub-

sonic vessels
they test

on
scaffolds

of foreign-

radars'
light; first

frost
repeating

in the mechanics

of the mouth
and the

sonograms
of these

antiquities'

revealing;

Assent Studies

early spring:
        and the ice-dams   in the sculptures' beards

raise water to their lips; and someone says there will be
another harvest if we can reach the fields
by May

someone agrees
someone agrees

to overlay their movements with video-feeds
to see who will enter

the transposed shops
        and clothe them; someone agrees

to the porous stone   of the pox

memorials;
and to wash the stone when families   come to pray;
someone agrees that this will keep

the pox

from spreading;
and someone agrees to the   dental-drill

engravings
        of their own

decay;

Anthem Speed

the standpipes flare
     and their vapor   signatures lengthen

into the flyways
     in dispersal plans;
     and the birds' bodies smell of smoke   and

river-
blindness

levels the mirage-trees;
     heat-capture devices
     and carbon-capture machines

and the literature on the lungs of chimney-sweeps
and the Vietnamese

factories
stitching our sleeves

shut

and our hands where   our hearts would be

     receiving pacemaker signals

from
other countries;

Prediction Monuments

the drug-
submarines leaching stimulants   into the sea;

and octopus ink tracing the veins of coral fans
        printing themselves

on eastward currents;
        as diagrams of the dye-tests

        of these   swimmers' lungs;

and the ghost ships' sonar screens   casting reefs
where captains' minds

would be;
and smugglers   shipping nails in nail-head

upholstery should the tsunami
need shrapnel

Attention in Statecraft Appendices

the
only word

was the leader's and birds—*quoting sky*
                                    with their movements—

were penned
in their aviaries

          whose gridded ground appeared in the landmine accords

the leader claimed to have based
                    on the gardens he saved from the war, saying,

the legacy of a leader is in his people's dreams

when everyone dreamt of walking, again, and, again, he cupped water
in his hands
and flung it

          and flared a fly's wings with steam

to fix
the

spider's gaze;

The Conference to Convene the Court

        we presented on *the climatic conditions of assassinations*
and on the terraria re-creating the conditions we found;

on contingencies for his or her survival, in the heat, and
the contingencies

for doctors in the crowds;
        we presented, equally, on the contingencies

of security teams—their plans to turn flags into litters—and
their flags

changing symbols

in forensic light

Transcript

I correspond with bots

       who play soccer with *the older boys*
and exist   at the edges of photographs
they send

of half-bodies about to strike a ball and *tear the net*

and would I fund its mending
and would I fund their mending
of window screens   their roommates

cut
to leave?—*while Petr* (a roommate's Christian name)
steals cigarettes

to clear

       his river walks   *of biting flies;*

Searching *The American West*

the bots posting lost rings to wedding chapel sites
        and posting herbal remedies to *the shortest wedding nights*;

and had I searched
        fungal infections affecting the bats in Wind Cave
                I would have burned my commemorative clothes

and the bots would be selling survival kits and
matches with weatherproof heads;

        a story would emerge   about *infected bats*
                responding to the *sounds of computer keys*

and the scientists' cataloging their *agitation at barrier screens*;
someone claims to have felt their form

being carried back
to these bats;

        and blames her lover for never speaking and the scientists
        for isolating *this*

self-
consciousness;

Production Values

the Russian bots will cast our *children*
in productions of   *America Live!*

      and place their lines on the sites our children
      search

and the first commercials will rehearse themselves
in your living-rooms

and the children will record them   for the bots assigned to their
cases

      and the bots will respond
      more quickly than the filters

I love America
and you and
I feel like I could cry and
can I use your web-cam light

to blink?

Dissident

the jailers call the trial runs of the execution   the *acoustic version*
of whatever

they hear when he dies; and

the Sisters who used to visit prisons   loop
film versions of themselves

undoing Ecclesiastes
in fewer and fewer words; and this

       is your anonymity number:
       and if I cross-list this number   with my own

we know who each other are
and will you tell them

they said this?

Search Graft

Today,
>   we found the searches our neighbors made
>   on our accounts

for *Russian brides* or *tactical gear*
or were they searching *Crimean* sites for their *sisters*

and their searches intercepted
and redirected to Russian dailies   whose

inserts are coated for wrapping fish
whose eyes   might lift the print

in redactions of Russian feats

which they preserve
on the same corneas
as

saw the net
too late;

Writs of Divisibility

the court will take depositions and
use biometric ballots

      to assign us
to decisions; and Earth will

be entered into evidence with
        the general's ascent

through the candidates' charts; and the fracking
quakes

drill cave floors
with stalactites;

and the first state
        sells mining rights to its cabling
and a second state

applies solar cells to its signs
(where words would be);

The Worker's Case

            history
is a series

of pretrial motions:
in the 27th hour a jury-room
painting

draws attention
to open fields and threshing sheds

appearing

at the same resolution as the crime-scene
photos

and the painter's deliberations: the
brush-stroke

metronome
moving them back and forth across the fields
and sub-
fields

of whatever they hear
in

each other's voices
pulsing the painting at

the field-
hand's

wrist;

The Achilles File

the agency's spectrometers   testing starlight for missile shade;

and other agencies intercepting an astronaut's blood-test
to trigger contamination protocols:

   to choreograph the live-feeds for their lovers
or their leaders

and distract us from the Earth's rotation
in the starboard window

as they plan   their future intercepts   of body-scans

to speed the bone-thinned beings
into earthbound crews

   and codename each operation
   by their

   injuries;

Reconstruction of

moving among
diagrams

of crimes
       with lasers

to light
the fires they set;

       an old trick
       to shine jury boxes

with watches
and let them

feel heat; to

sequence evidence
       that ends

       by calling a name; to
model the world

in the absence
of someone they know;

and let it

spin, mechanically,
cutting the air

with
its

monuments;

Protocols

they practice finding wash stations
they practice bagging clothes in a chamber and checking
another chamber's seal
they practice pressing intercoms and identifying absences
      in the third chamber
and begin to count themselves
into fourth chamber
groups
where they receive assignments for the fifth chamber
or assignments for former chambers where they fog the glass
to hide whichever chamber
jails the thief;

Hunger Scaffold

you unwind the gauze from my head and each
blot of blood

        orbits between us—   as images of planets

growing stronger—
and you suggest I name one for a lover I remember

     (to test me on her name)

and needles etch
lesser planets

        into biohazard bins;
        and their cataract moons

appear—
in which phase

of this disease?—
to eclipse   the faces

of the names
I call;

The Evolution of Signs

in the notes (in the Latin) it said 'saint with shovel' and what lay
unearthed was another saint whose hands were clasped
around fragments;

above the fish-
scuttled shores:

the weather reports   reprinting themselves, in spring snow,

and maps bleeding
against   lost climbers, in the thaw

and loose snow   lisping across the rock

and moonlight against the mountains
and the horizon's grammar

imprinting
the animal young;

Conduction Rifts

when the ports closed,

the cruise-ship governments (their doctors
                rising quickly through their ranks)

sanctioned every marriage tying them

to land; and

their desalination plants
earned easements to run their pipes ashore;

as trash-packs near the intake burned:
                heating bilge-water and fogging the steerage

mirrors
where children learned to write
words

that would not last; and their

ships, melting the oceans' weave

archiving the sea
in its amber,

                and shifting
                prosthetic islands,   above islands

lost;
and their peoples piping rain

through the raised arms of plastic dolls
whose grips

tighten in the sun,
                the people claim,

when the aqueduct

runs dry;

The Spillway Meditations

the flooded fields   fermenting
and geese
drunkenly chasing   reflected geese   from water-

thinned nests—
and the companies claiming the sugar-beet pickers have been clapping

their hands—
and the   automated plows

have been tallying the rotations of their disks
through anomalies

      to identify
      soapstone talismans

whose mouths
they opened

for this singing;

Dominion Claim

the night they went to bless the canyons, their hands

were raised by updrafts—

from the guano-heated caves—
and they blessed the other side;

and they tried, again,   to bless the canyons
and the updrafts raised their hands

and their god   blessed other gods

with absolution
for their men;

and the sandstorms lined the canyons
with cavalries

and their flood-
rusted sabers

ran, briefly,
through the pictographs'

grasp;

Borderlands II

this translation application says that you 'love (me)' and that you
'exiled (your) brother'

      and that the hill he climbed was 'latticed' with the 'elevations
      on our screens'

and that 'we should not look up'
until 'he reaches the pines': that

      now he is 'burning boughs to scent our clothes
      and signal *who*'

      you wonder
      and 'would they know the direction of the wind'

and should we 'double-back or light a fire for ourselves'
or for whichever 'neighbors

arrive to console us' as you repeat yourself to them and   the translation
application

says you 'love (me)' and you '*exalted*
(your) brother'

and the neighbors' chatter
lights the screen

with translations of their invectives
against *which*

smoke

Dominion Song

the billboard theology
we study

from trains
where someone makes

digital

claims
to the lambs

in the field
below;

while Armed
Forces Radio

connects this
"longtime listener,"

to his
own voice;

and a radio chaplain
holds

a service for his dead

and we
use our silence

Concentricity

in the fields,

      we cut the prescriptions' shine by rubbing pills with our hands;
and the wind-scattered casings

dissolve
in blackbirds' nests

      dappling the ground with light;

and the trace
amounts

in the birds' bones   would numb the wolves' mouths
and their gums would bleed when they broke

the trough-ice
to drink

and the small plumes of their blood turned them
on the collared male

      whose transmissions
           continue

from beyond

        which radius?

State Rooms

and
the sections of bog

cut from shore
to infest the ships

with flies; and
a single flower's

single mark
accents

a ship's name

and the language
change

        defames
        the president's uncle

and the ports are closed
and passengers

cannot
tour the tunnels

        or fold
        landmine memorials

        into origami

craters
as their ships'

chaplains had
folded   illuminated pages

to extend

Christ's hands
through

sinners' hair;

Crenulations of Future Fires

and the algorithms we ran for heat
    solved too quickly

                    to thaw the machines;

and the algorithms for decorative scrolls
        appearing on dignitaries' screens

and their delight when their screens'
static flashed

against their hands
or their uniform pins   enameled themselves in the static blasts

and hardened the leading edge
of each symbol's

sword

or hardened the hammers
of the labor-

camp commandants
requesting the algorithm for the depth,   the Earth

would cauterize
their

miners' wounds;

Figure Studies

the workers never returning to conversations

they started
      with the union-

hall
projecting their names
          to the docks
            and the trawlers scattering rough-fish

      during the slurring

of a Dutch name
and the trawlers' workers never
              looking up from their knives

to amplify
      the Dutchman's

complaint
allowing
          the barnacle lines of the dry-docked ships

      to model
      whose perception

      removing nothing

from the rain, in the shipyards, collecting it
as an object

Field Guide

the flora in statecraft appendices   *for camouflaging foreign forces*;

or training insects
to hatch

a listening device

     in a *funeral arrangement of
violets;*

     and your seamstress reporting runs   on *the patterns
your gardens would hide*

     and the exiled battalions   using your bands to smuggle brass

and your foundries flaring
to form casings   your countrymen fire:

and doors flying open   and *the blooms of hothouse flowers*

erasing
your surrender

     from the window-
steam;

Algorithms of Obsolescence

        the uranium mines thinning quail eggs
in arcs around their openings;

and the skull of a desert fox   chattering its isotopic teeth
through

Geiger counters;
and the first flush of fledglings   across the mountainside

the scientists cross
to cage their cancerous mice   in *therapeutic range*;

      and their single-use radios   relaying coordinates to their assistants

or wrapped to capture sounds of their absence
         or of caves fluting in the distance

      with wastewater deepening their tones
and a single work-light   still swinging in their mouths

still signaling   *inward* or *outward*

to the valley's other side
the speed

of their half-lives;

The Union of Cause

planetary rings
            fused particles from passing comets
and cratered the planets with ore;

and we began to organize by the hours of the other
planets' days;

        we were the union of metal workers
                    as the waters rose with metal-

heavy fish
and alloys of brain and bone

pinned them to the shoals;
            and the longshoremen pieced cranes
                        from cranes without controls

and scanned freighters with lasers:

beaming numbers back and forth
in tallies of the ships   they would never land

or in tallies
of the deckhands

they blinded;

Lunar Years

de-
programmers work the trigger-scents

of captors' gardens

and captors' food;
     the hostage recalls the flash-
     grenade

as the god of her extraction; and
     families are allowed two memories

from each session:
and you choose the rivers where fish-

ladders allow the sun   to cast salmon shadows
across the cliffs

as pictographs
and days spent spinning
        fruit—by its stems—

to speed the crescents
your fingernails
left,

in its skins;

Soundwave

muskoxen   scared from the rivers' shores
test

the tundra's thaw; and the shearing of their wool by children
light-
        enough to reach them

and the mapping of their fossils' fuels
for future nations'

leaders
and lease terms

        raising micro-wells against the midnight sun;
the tar-pits'   respiration rates
measured

        in the distance between their rings
and the satellite imaging

capturing patterns for the records
these future nations

play—

remember us;

Coordinates

they claim the collaborators

        loosened the mares

of the carousels   and drove their hooves
against the ground

and deafened the worker or the worker's son

       who watched the horse he'd carved   split a hoof
       (the knotted wood

had shod it)
and told its startled rider   that its wormwood mane

flared
eastward when he found it

and the *west wind* he'd envisioned
drove the horse

toward
this

ringing   in his ears;

Lot 29

the life-
flights

       control their patients' pressures

with altitude; above crops
      engineered

to dye the migrants' hands;
        above

          auction-bidding

on
civil-war
     dentures—

'chipped by powder-horns—having been driven

battle by battle
into the

shine'; above
the soldiers' sketches

         of their generals

         cascading across the fields;
above the serial-numbers

       in the shrapnel

and the blood-
stamped

surgeon's tray;

Omen Ecology

when the wolves fell ill, we cultured
                    the camera lenses

                in the animals' dens;

                                began to film ourselves;

and the geysers' turbines mineralized
into stone-age

blades;
when people gutted the mechanical bull   in the Cooke

City bar
for ventilator

parts;

the paramedics held their hands
                        above their patients

and the washboard roads
compressed their chests;

when
I couldn't stop thinking about the fluid
in my knee

I became

encephalitic;
            this is the thermocline

I can't
raise my head

to reach;

Decertification

we could smell the docents
           folding   the spice-ships' sails

in the East Wing;
these are their dissertations
                         on *moths tunneling through tarot*
decks
for the beet-dye coloring
               the reaper's sickle; this is their table—

with its dissections
of moths

into red and mauve

parts—reconstructing contact made; and the solutions

they test on their wings
           to tinge the tiles beneath skylights
           these shades

of
workers' blood

Photo Enhancements

the civilians in unnamed wars
                    swept through fruit groves and corn fields;

        and these are his chevrons of colored cloth
dyeing their jewelry box;

why has it rained in Toledo and the smokestacks not come clean
why has it rained in Toronto and the river not broken its banks;

if the union should break its lines—
            will you identify your father's friend

                             from the line-up they provide
when it becomes July—and the milk cartons sweat
and their

missing
persons weep—

History Vector

here is a nobleman's daughter and her corset's bones
broken for marrow

      to calm the strays . . .
      here are revolutionaries raising checkpoints
         to check papers

for the warmth of those arriving from afar

      or the warmth of those running
from the square; there are lines behind barrels

used as tables
      and their papers' names struck with coal;

women
standing clear of their lines

      wondering what the barrels once held
when a horse appears—rider-less—

a saber slapping against its saddle

      and the men leave their barrels to click their tongues
as their colonels had—

      when threshers scattered or fell silent in threshers' shacks—

      or as radiomen had when their colonels claimed
our mice are crushed by the weight of our wheat:

and the rebels'
false-

bottomed barrels
are

      tainted by blood;

Leaderless Songs

studies sketched on moleskin erase the studies below;
or soften the studies' hands—

                           where they clutched what you wanted—

and shift the bird's attention

to the *viewers'* hands
          and claim the dimensions broken

as your own;
and what would have slowed the chimney-sweeps—

to exactly this speed,
          between us—with ember-clotted holes in their sleeves—

          and slowed their delivery of the chimney-
          swallows' nests

we fired in December—
          their interiors   fissure-marked by April's

fissured eggs—   and their openings

as fretted—*by feathered trembling*—
as the

convalescents'
tunneled light?

Pier-Filtered Voices

the pearl-
clatter

       in the currents

carrying
oysters

       and the moon
       raising

       its decibels
       above the shore

where refugees
assimilate
       near the rivers'

       mouths, and leave
       their dead

agate-

eyed
and recite
       aphorisms

about the manger's
creatures

       for local
       patrols

and sing—
       of the myrrh-
       scarred mouths,

       of the desert wolves

trailing
these kings;

Agency Identifications

they say the lucky man
                    hangs clothes from assassins' darts

and the darts' poison   stops mice nesting in the wall; that

          the first raindrop accents the extradition

order's name
and they must allow him a stay;

they say the fruit stand is not a fruit stand
        but a way to scent the smugglers' crates; they say

the lucky man reveals the smugglers' names
and affixes tracking devices   they made to look like nails; they say

conspiracy leaflets

take fingerprints, too; but the lucky man exists online—
as *operational*

asset number five—funding

funerals
to snarl the capital with

processionals;

Blood Values

the infirmary measures swelling
                    by the turns of the halos'

screws; and the nurses attend

            the shadow

coronations
of their patients, each dawn;   the locked wards unlock themselves

with access cards

they magnetize
            on cupboard catches;

this rationing, *this*

bypassing breathing tubes
                    through the hollow handrails

of the hospital beds

lengthens
the

ventilators'

            reach

Fuel-Tested Future

the altar of moon rock assembled
                         as memorial to its surface, untouched;

retired
cosmonauts on Soviet-era balconies

picturing the altar-
               shadow

consecrating
un-

tenanted
ground

             of which beliefs—
the future will broadcast to

itself
and follow to the buffalo-

                    jump fossils
                    and picture them

                              midflight

resembling the relics left
weightlessly

             above the altar;

Metrics for Autonomy

the Defense Department tracks language proficiency in
its prisoners

        to determine where its guard-dogs will train;
on windy days advanced teams collect

the infection rates,
the schoolyards' trash confirms (and these dogs can be used,

        per these contracts,
        in the valleys of their handlers' births

until
such time as hostilities cease) and

the language-school texts
                include the word for *vaccine*

in their lessons on future-tense, or in
                their conversations

           predicting
           the future of French

        or France,

where scientists conclude   the lesions on bats' brains
are stealth-

encounters;

Transcription Services

ten thousand marching soldiers pulse the aquifer's chambers—
the bunkers

built on industrial springs—
        the radius of wells their enemies use;

            and the invasion algorithms involve *pipeline* searches
            on German-language sites;   and Ukrainian woodsmen split wood

            for wormwood hieroglyphs
            of escape

            or wormwood hieroglyphs
                of trenching the Eastern front

where soldiers secure the conservatories—   *"lest the students turn*

3D printers into
caches of

concealable guns"—and release the false-flag recordings

of Ukrainians singing *"to keep from sounding*

their floorboards
through

hidden rooms";

Choreography Notations

when I was in prison
                    I joined the eighth human ladder

            that formed;

and assembled the ninth ladder
to join

            another prison's first and raise

a cathedral's arch;
the prisoners working laundry embroidered sheets

with the

            prison wall's pattern
            to cloak the ladder's base; and

artificial intelligence
estimates animal activity,

seismologically,   and logged the seventh ladder

under *horsemanship*; and the actors

            in Milgram's experiments
            were classically trained; and

in the prophesy
the arch's apex will hold

the
martyrs'

embrace;

Litigation

when the courts will not compel the samples: we run the suspects
through tick-riddled fields;

       our hands are white from bleaching coral guides;
cherry blossoms ferry their fragrance across the puddles and

data migration
captures the executioners' streams and their accomplices

selling virtual spots in firing lines
          as prisoners blink code to the caches of bitcoin

     the hackers mine
     with air-defense servers to raise the single-

     link satellites
     that prove

     they loved;

Exhibition 2.0

another docent claims,
       the scepter's prints are from whichever servant saw the king

       clutch his chest;
       the depth of his prints points to wearing

rough cloth and carving
       fatty meats—that the king's trusting him

with such knives
would mean his lifting the scepter, would not

have seen him hung:
and the docent will check the songs for whether or not his

imprisonment
included sons; and the war

in Basquiat
is without foxes to hunt to clothe its soldiers: and rats

that climbed the labyrinths of paint
might shed a single

glove's-worth

to warm the painter's hand
and keep his fingerprints

from his subjects'
teeth;

Protocol 2.1

the brooch should be light enough to beat its wings to the wearer's heart-
beat: stitching and re-stitching its shadow on their chest;   and its

light should blind the extraction teams that do not know the codes; and
if you do not speak the language,

the numbers will be offered on radio dials; and if you do not speak the language,
negotiations will require a local

      and you can offer him the machine
          designed to deliver the hostage meals   and demonstrate

its ability   to negotiate stairs
and let his children load it with meats for their father and let his wife

view him through its eyes; let his sister
turn it on herself, to watch herself sing; and let the hologram,

sent to instruct the hostage, present her with its key; and let its heat
brand the *hostage's* hand

      with the form they will need for their shackles;

ACKNOWLEDGMENTS

MANY THANKS to Mark Levine and Emily Wilson for the vision and guidance offered in ushering this book into being. Thank you to the Central Minnesota Arts Board for the grant that supported the writing of these poems. And thank you, *North American Review* ("The Spillway Meditations") and *Meridian* ("Soundwave"), for publishing poems from this collection.

KUHL HOUSE POETS

Christopher Bolin
Anthem Speed

Christopher Bolin
Ascension Theory

Christopher Bolin
Form from Form

Shane Book
Congotronic

Oni Buchanan
Must a Violence

Oni Buchanan
Time Being

Michele Glazer
fretwork

Michele Glazer
On Tact, & the Made Up World

David Micah Greenberg
Planned Solstice

Jeff Griffin
Lost and

Hajar Hussaini
Disbound

John Isles
Ark

John Isles
Inverse Sky

Aaron McCollough
Rank

Randall Potts
Trickster

Bin Ramke
Airs, Waters, Places

Bin Ramke
Matter

Michelle Robinson
The Life of a Hunter

Vanessa Roveto
bodys

Vanessa Roveto
a women

Robyn Schiff
Revolver

Robyn Schiff
Worth

Sarah V. Schweig
Take Nothing with You

Rod Smith
Deed

Donna Stonecipher
Transaction Histories

Cole Swensen
The Book of a Hundred Hands

Cole Swensen
Such Rich Hour

Tony Tost
Complex Sleep

Pimone Triplett
Supply Chain

Nick Twemlow
Attributed to the Harrow Painter

Susan Wheeler
Meme

Emily Wilson
The Keep